Animal Migrations
Reptile Migration

by Carollyne Hutter

FOCUS
READERS.

BEACON

www.focusreaders.com

Focus Readers is distributed by North Star Editions:
sales@northstareditions.com | 888-417-0195

Produced for Focus Readers by Red Line Editorial.

Photographs ©: Shutterstock Images, cover, 1, 4, 7, 8, 11, 13, 14, 17, 19, 22, 25, 27, 29; John Sullivan/Alamy, 20–21

Library of Congress Cataloging-in-Publication Data
Names: Hutter, Carollyne, author.
Title: Reptile migration / by Carollyne Hutter.
Description: Lake Elmo, MN : Focus Readers, [2024] | Series: Animal
   migrations | Includes bibliographical references and index. | Audience:
   Grades 2-3
Identifiers: LCCN 2023008348 (print) | LCCN 2023008349 (ebook) | ISBN
   9781637396094 (hardcover) | ISBN 9781637396667 (paperback) | ISBN
   9781637397770 (pdf) | ISBN 9781637397237 (ebook)
Subjects: LCSH: Reptiles--Migration--Juvenile literature.
Classification: LCC QL644.2 .H885 2024 (print) | LCC QL644.2 (ebook) |
   DDC 597.9156/8--dc23/eng/20230322
LC record available at https://lccn.loc.gov/2023008348
LC ebook record available at https://lccn.loc.gov/2023008349

Printed in the United States of America
Mankato, MN
082023

About the Author

Carollyne Hutter writes for children and adults on science, geography, and the environment. She finds these fields fascinating and is always learning. She has written eight books and more than 25 magazine articles for children, covering such topics as rain forests, the weather, oceans, the arts, African wildlife, and more.

Table of Contents

Chapter 1

Turtle Travels

A leatherback sea turtle swims in the Caribbean Sea. She makes her way to an island. The turtle crawls onto the beach. She digs a hole in the sand. Then she lays eggs in the hole. She covers them with sand.

 A leatherback sea turtle can lay more than 100 eggs at a time.

Two months later, baby turtles hatch from the eggs. But their mother is gone.

After laying her eggs, the mother turtle begins her long **migration**. She swims north. The turtle reaches the cold waters of Canada. She finds many jellyfish to eat. They

Fun Fact

Leatherback sea turtles migrate farther than any other reptile. They swim up to 10,000 miles (16,000 km) every year.

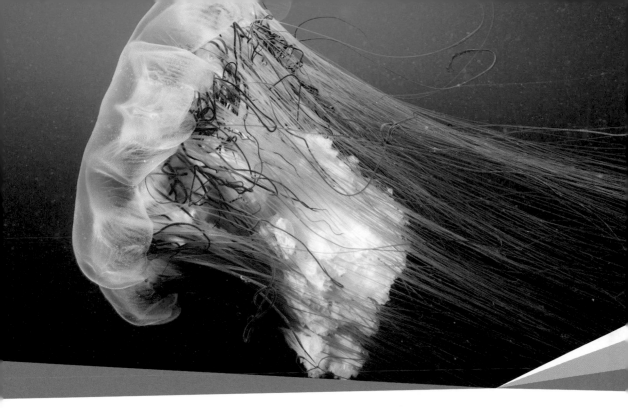

 Leatherback sea turtles can eat dozens of jellyfish every day.

give the turtle energy to stay warm and keep moving.

The mother turtle swims around the ocean for years. Then, she returns to her nesting grounds. She will repeat her journey.

Chapter 2

Sea Turtle Migration

Some turtles live in water. Others live on land. Land turtles stay close to where they were born. But sea turtles travel long distances every year. Sea turtles can swim well. Their legs are like large paddles.

 Sea turtles live in many parts of the ocean, including coral reefs.

Sea turtles cross oceans to find food. They also travel to find **mates** and places to nest.

Loggerhead sea turtles swim out to sea after they hatch. Then they spend up to 15 years in the open ocean. Loggerheads have powerful jaws. They use them to break the shells of crabs.

When loggerheads are fully grown, they migrate. They swim back to the beaches where they were born. That is where they mate.

Sea turtles can hold their breath for more than an hour.

Some loggerheads travel nearly 8,000 miles (13,000 km).

Green sea turtles spend most of their lives in areas near coasts.

There they can search for food. They eat algae and seagrass. But every two to five years, green sea turtles migrate. They swim to nesting beaches to lay eggs.

Sea turtles can travel thousands of miles in the open ocean. And somehow, they always find the same beach. Scientists are not sure

Fun Fact

Sea turtles ride ocean waves and follow **currents**. That helps them save energy.

> **Only 1 in 1,000 baby sea turtles survives to adulthood.**

how they do it. Sea turtles may be able to sense Earth's **magnetic field**. That could help the turtles find their way.

Chapter 3

Snake Migration

Some snakes migrate to different areas during the summer and winter. They go to certain places when it gets hotter or colder. These snakes migrate to find food. They also migrate to **hibernate**.

Cottonmouth snakes migrate from swamps in the summer to forests in the winter.

Garter snakes in Canada migrate every year. In the summer, the snakes live in areas where they can find food. Then they spend the winter in dens. The dens are underground. That way, garter snakes can stay below the frost line. This is the area where the ground

Fun Fact

Garter snakes usually share a den. More than 10,000 snakes may use the same den.

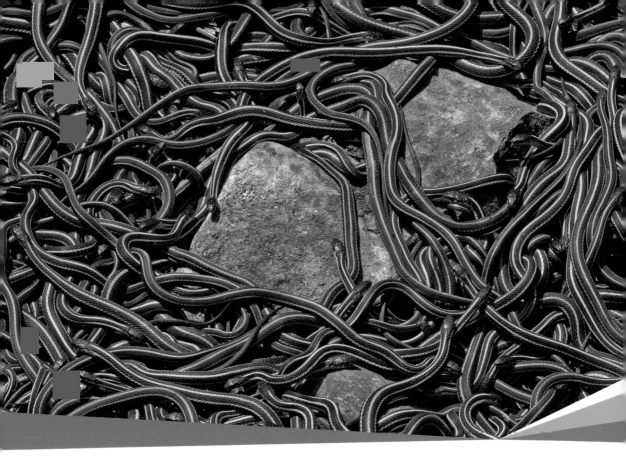

> Tens of thousands of garter snakes migrate near Narcisse, Manitoba.

does not freeze. Staying below the frost line keeps the garter snakes warm. They hibernate through the winter. In spring, the garter snakes slither back up to the surface.

Some snakes in the tropics also migrate. These snakes do not hibernate. That's because the tropics don't get cold in the winter. But some parts of the year have lots of rain. Other parts are dry. So, the snakes may have to travel to find food or water.

Arafura file snakes live in Australia and other nearby countries. These snakes stay in shallow ponds during the dry season. Nearby grasslands and

 Arafura file snakes are known for their loose skin.

mangroves become flooded during the wet season. The snakes migrate to the flooded areas. They can hunt for food there.

Water Pythons

Water pythons live in Australia and other nearby areas. These snakes eat small animals. They kill their **prey** by squeezing.

Fogg Dam is a wilderness area in northern Australia. Here, water pythons often eat rats. Every year, rains cause the area to flood. So, the rats have to move to higher ground. Many water pythons follow the rats. The snakes migrate up to 7.5 miles (12 km) to go after their food.

Water pythons usually grow to lengths of 7 feet (2.1 m).

Chapter 4

Lizards and Crocodiles

Most lizards do not migrate. They stay in the same area their whole lives. But some lizards do travel short distances. Galápagos land iguanas are one example. They live on islands near South America.

 Galápagos land iguanas can weigh up to 29 pounds (13 kg).

Females migrate every year. They travel up to 9 miles (15 km) to their nesting grounds. They find sandy areas where they can lay their eggs.

Iguana migration also happens in Panama. Female green iguanas migrate in January and February. They travel nearly 2 miles (3 km) to nest. Many iguanas swim to an island together. They lay eggs there. Then they return to the mainland.

Most alligators and crocodiles do not migrate either. But some move

> **Green iguanas spend much of their time in trees.**

around throughout the year. They look for nesting spots or areas with more water.

Nile crocodiles live in many parts of Africa. They nest in the same places each year. Some Nile crocodiles in South Africa migrate a short distance. They relocate from rivers and lakes to nearby **floodplains**. They look for places to nest with good soil and shade.

Fun Fact

Saltwater crocodiles are the largest reptiles on Earth. Males can grow up to 16 feet (4.9 m) long.

 On hot days, crocodiles keep their mouths open to stay cool.

Saltwater crocodiles live in parts of Australia and Asia. They stay in **estuaries** during the dry season. Then they move to swamps and rivers for the wet season.

FOCUS ON
Reptile Migration

Write your answers on a separate piece of paper.

1. Write a paragraph describing the main ideas of Chapter 3.

2. What type of reptile migration do you think is most interesting? Why?

3. Which reptile has the longest migration?
   - **A.** leatherback sea turtle
   - **B.** Nile crocodile
   - **C.** garter snake

4. Why might green iguanas travel to an island to lay eggs?
   - **A.** so the babies are far from danger
   - **B.** so the babies will not survive
   - **C.** so the babies can't get back to the mainland

5. What does **tropics** mean in this book?

*Some snakes in the **tropics** also migrate. These snakes do not hibernate. That's because the tropics don't get cold in the winter.*

    A. places where animals are always safe
    B. places that are usually warm and wet
    C. places where snakes are unable to survive

6. What does **relocate** mean in this book?

*Some Nile crocodiles in South Africa migrate a short distance. They **relocate** from rivers and lakes to nearby floodplains.*

    A. to sink in deep waters
    B. to stay in the same place
    C. to move to a new place

Answer key on page 32.

Glossary

currents
Water movements that go in a certain direction.

estuaries
Areas where rivers or streams flow into the ocean.

floodplains
Areas near rivers that often become flooded.

hibernate
To save energy by resting or sleeping during a season.

magnetic field
The space around an object (such as a moon or planet) in which its magnetic force can be detected.

mangroves
Types of trees or plants that grow in coastal areas where fresh water and salt water mix.

mates
Partners that have babies together.

migration
The movement of a group of animals from one place to another.

prey
Animals that are hunted and eaten by other animals.

To Learn More

BOOKS

Jopp, Kelsey. *Leatherback Sea Turtle Migration.*
Lake Elmo, MN: Focus Readers, 2019.

MacCarald, Clara. *Migrating to Survive.*
Minneapolis: Abdo Publishing, 2023.

Markle, Sandra. *On the Hunt with Crocodiles.*
Minneapolis: Lerner Publications, 2023.

NOTE TO EDUCATORS

Visit **www.focusreaders.com** to find lesson plans, activities, links, and other resources related to this title.

Index

A
alligators, 24–25
Arafura file snakes, 18–19

C
crocodiles, 24–27
currents, 12

G
Galápagos land iguanas, 23–24
garter snakes, 16–17
green iguanas, 24
green sea turtles, 11–12

H
hibernation, 15, 17–18

J
jellyfish, 6–7

L
leatherback sea turtles, 5–7
lizards, 23–24
loggerhead sea turtles, 10–11

M
magnetic fields, 13

N
Nile crocodiles, 26

S
saltwater crocodiles, 26–27
sea turtles, 5–7, 9–13
snakes, 15–19, 20

W
water pythons, 20

Answer Key: 1. Answers will vary; **2.** Answers will vary; **3.** A; **4.** A; **5.** B; **6.** C